Body Books

Breathing

Anna Sandeman
Illustrated by Ian Thompson

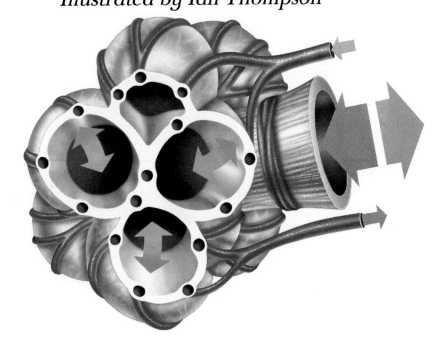

COPPER BEECH BOOKS

BROOKFIELD, CONNECTICUT

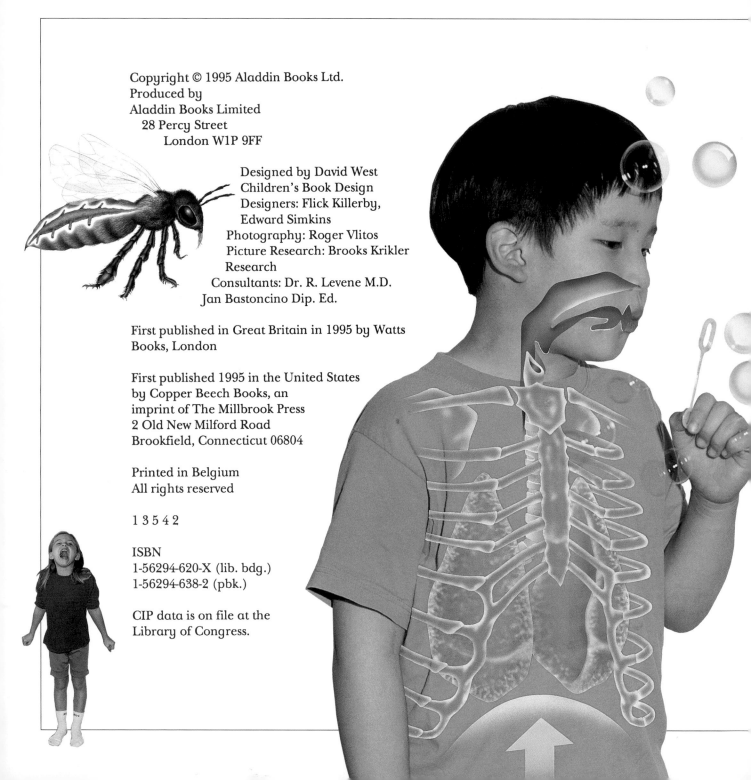

Copyright © 1995 Aladdin Books Ltd.
Produced by
Aladdin Books Limited
28 Percy Street
London W1P 9FF

Designed by David West
Children's Book Design
Designers: Flick Killerby,
Edward Simkins
Photography: Roger Vlitos
Picture Research: Brooks Krikler
Research
Consultants: Dr. R. Levene M.D.
Jan Bastoncino Dip. Ed.

First published in Great Britain in 1995 by Watts
Books, London

First published 1995 in the United States
by Copper Beech Books, an
imprint of The Millbrook Press
2 Old New Milford Road
Brookfield, Connecticut 06804

Printed in Belgium

1 3 5 4 2

ISBN
1-56294-620-X (lib. bdg.)
1-56294-638-2 (pbk.)

CIP data is on file at the
Library of Congress.

Contents

Who breathes?

Almost all animals have to breathe to stay alive. Different animals breathe in different ways. This depends partly on where they live, and partly on their size.

Amphibians live both in water and on land. They breathe through their skin and with their lungs.

An insect is so small it needs only a simple network of tubes to carry air around its body.

A fish breathes through sieve-like gills on its sides.

Larger land-living animals, including humans, depend on powerful lungs to suck in all the air they need.

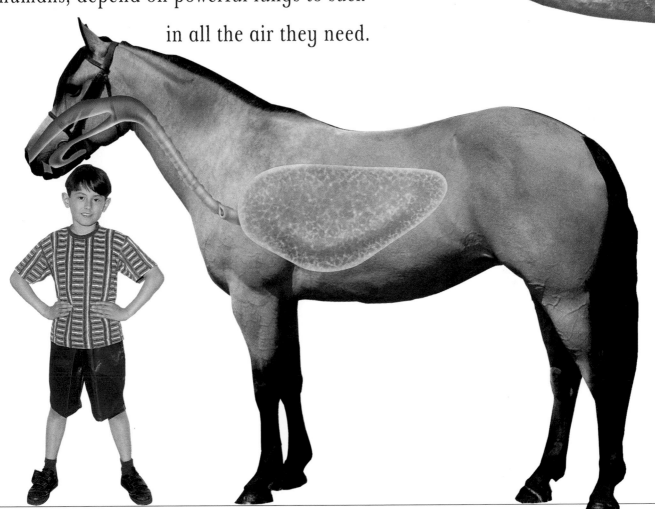

Where are your lungs?

You have two lungs, one on each side of your chest. The left lung is smaller than the right to leave room for your heart! If you could touch your lungs, they would feel soft and spongy.

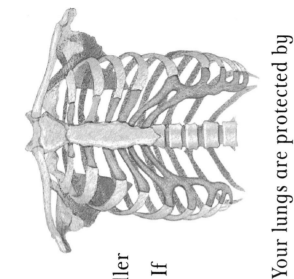

Just below your lungs is a large sheet of muscle called the diaphragm. This is a kind of wall between your lungs and the rest of your trunk. Like your rib muscles, your diaphragm tightens and relaxes as you breathe in and out.

Your lungs are protected by your rib cage. This is formed by twelve pairs of ribs which curve around from your backbone to meet up at the front. Muscles between your ribs tighten and relax to allow your rib cage to move.

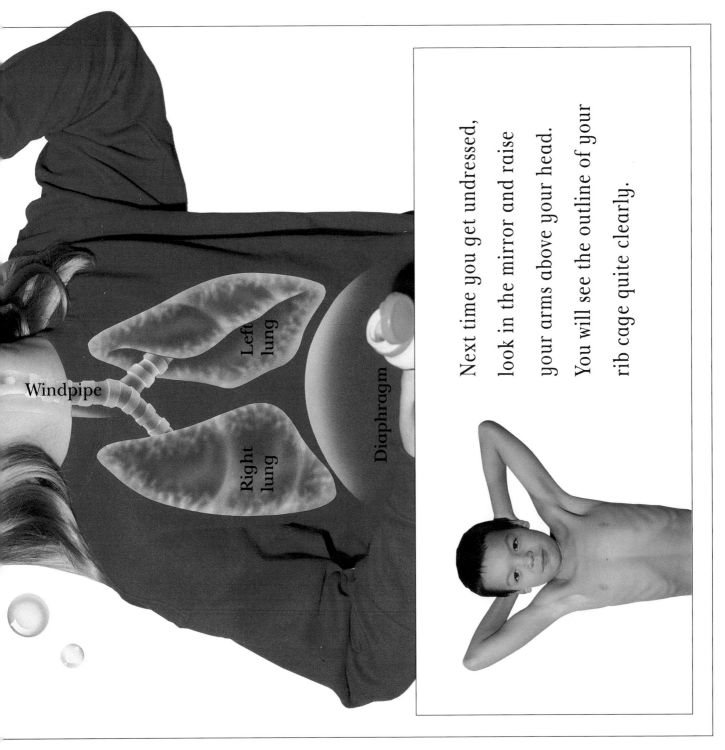

Windpipe

Left lung

Right lung

Diaphragm

Next time you get undressed, look in the mirror and raise your arms above your head. You will see the outline of your rib cage quite clearly.

Inside your lungs

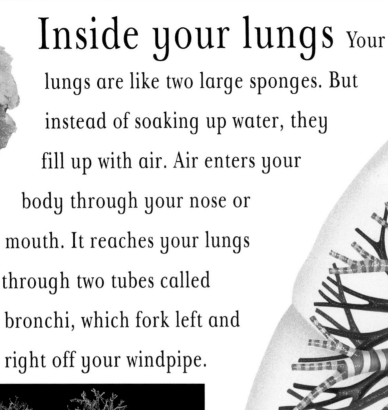

Your lungs are like two large sponges. But instead of soaking up water, they fill up with air. Air enters your body through your nose or mouth. It reaches your lungs through two tubes called bronchi, which fork left and right off your windpipe.

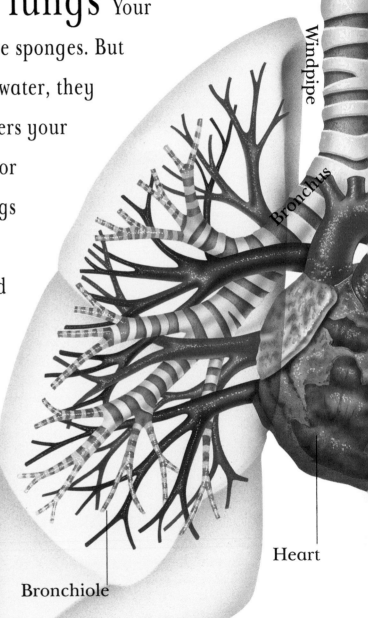

Windpipe

Bronchus

Heart

Bronchiole

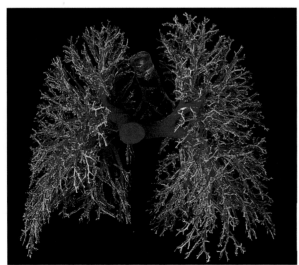

This model shows the bronchi and bronchioles in a pair of lungs.

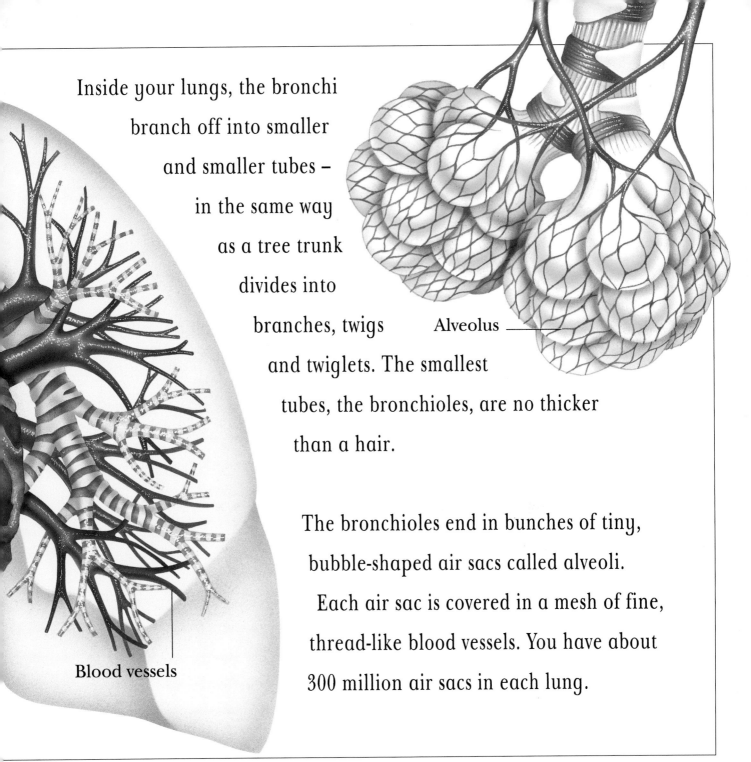

Inside your lungs, the bronchi branch off into smaller and smaller tubes – in the same way as a tree trunk divides into branches, twigs and twiglets. The smallest tubes, the bronchioles, are no thicker than a hair.

Alveolus

The bronchioles end in bunches of tiny, bubble-shaped air sacs called alveoli. Each air sac is covered in a mesh of fine, thread-like blood vessels. You have about 300 million air sacs in each lung.

Blood vessels

Why do you breathe?

Your body needs a gas called oxygen to stay alive. Oxygen is one of several gases in our air. When you breathe air into your lungs, oxygen passes through the thin walls of the air sacs and into your blood. Your heart pumps the blood and oxygen around your body.

Inside you oxygen mixes with a sugar called glucose.

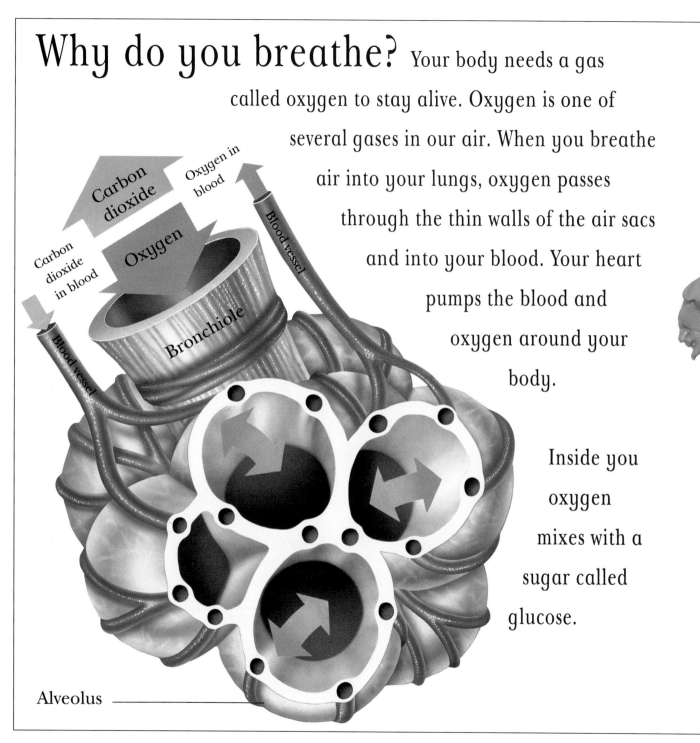

Carbon dioxide

Oxygen in blood

Carbon dioxide in blood

Oxygen

Blood vessel

Bronchiole

Blood vessel

Alveolus

Glucose comes from your food. Mixed together, oxygen and glucose produce energy. Energy helps you to run races, play football – or do anything else you ask of your body.

When energy is made, water and a gas called carbon dioxide are produced. These are not wanted by your body, so your blood carries them back to your lungs, ready to leave your body when you breathe out.

Breathing in

When you need to take a breath, your diaphragm tightens and moves down. Your rib muscles also tighten, forcing your ribs to move up and out. There is now more space in your chest, and air rushes in to fill it.

Put your hand on your chest. You can feel your ribs move with each breath.

Breathe out as far as you can. Ask a friend to measure your chest. Next take a deep breath in. How big is your chest now?

Air is sucked into your nose or mouth, down your throat and into your windpipe. From here it goes through the bronchi and the bronchioles, and into the air sacs. The air sacs fill up with air and your lungs expand.

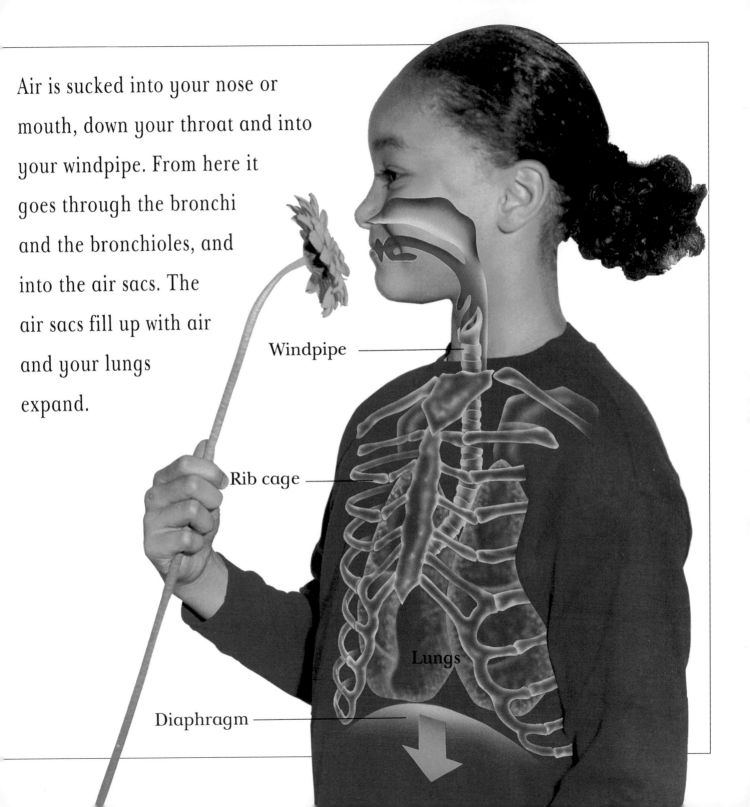

Windpipe

Rib cage

Lungs

Diaphragm

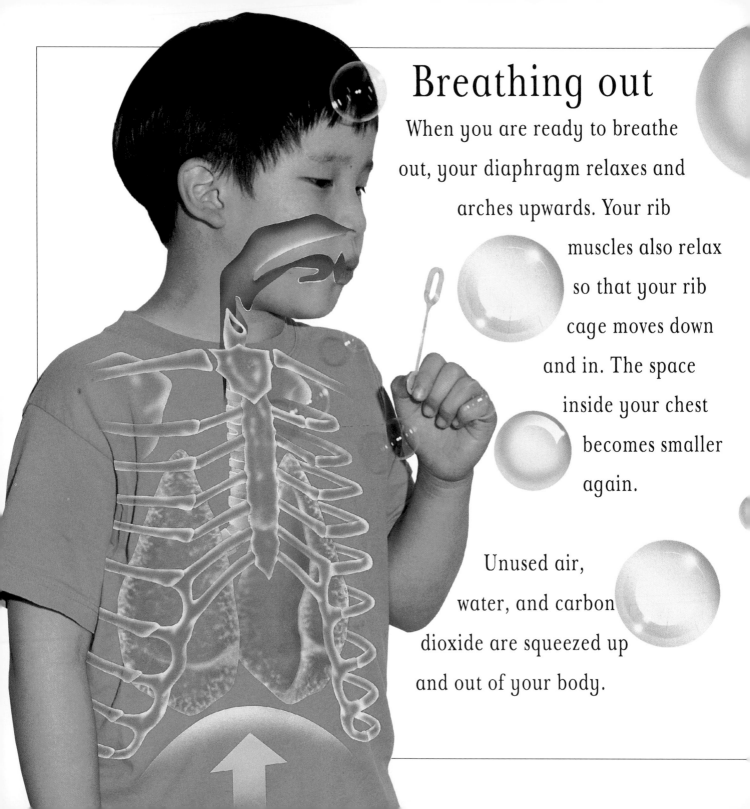

Breathing out

When you are ready to breathe out, your diaphragm relaxes and arches upwards. Your rib muscles also relax so that your rib cage moves down and in. The space inside your chest becomes smaller again.

Unused air, water, and carbon dioxide are squeezed up and out of your body.

Air that you breathe out carries heat from the warm inner parts of your body. You can feel how warm it is if you cup your hands over your mouth as you breathe out.

See for yourself the water that is in the air you breathe out. Put a small mirror in the refrigerator for about an hour. Wipe it and hold it in front of your mouth as you breathe out. The water in your breath becomes a fog of droplets on the cold mirror.

Breathing rapidly and slowly

Listen to your breathing. If you are sitting or lying down it is probably soft, slow and even. Count how many breaths you take in one minute.

One slow breath takes five seconds.

In 24 hours you breathe in nearly 2,200 gallons (10,000 liters) of air – enough to fill 30,000 cans! You breathe in a third of that at night, as your body is resting and does not need so much energy.

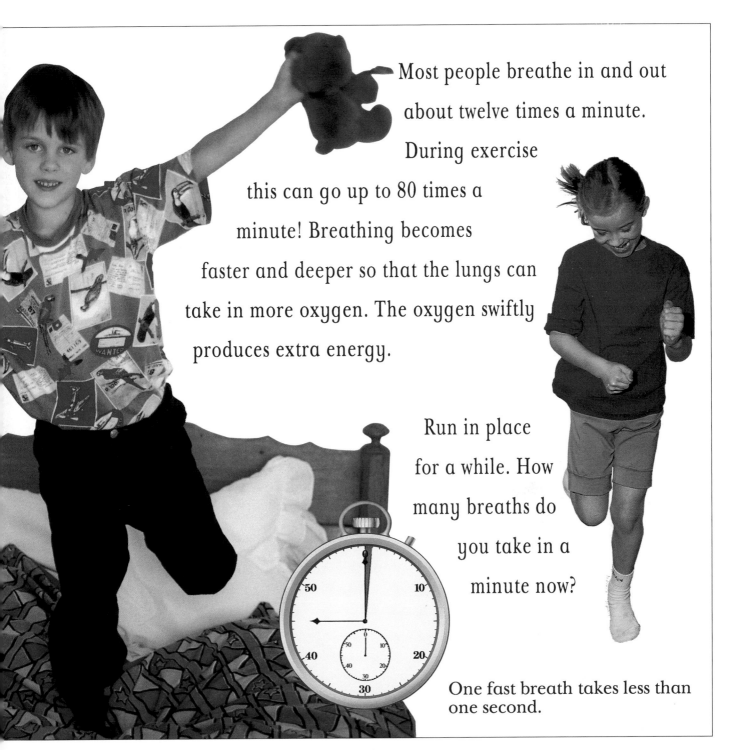

Most people breathe in and out about twelve times a minute. During exercise this can go up to 80 times a minute! Breathing becomes faster and deeper so that the lungs can take in more oxygen. The oxygen swiftly produces extra energy.

Run in place for a while. How many breaths do you take in a minute now?

One fast breath takes less than one second.

The air around you

Only about one fifth of Earth's air is oxygen. Much of the rest is nitrogen. Above 5,000 feet (1,500 meters) or so, air becomes thinner and contains less oxygen. At this height your lungs would have to struggle to take in more oxygen. Mountaineers who go higher than 5,000 feet often take their own supply of oxygen to help them breathe.

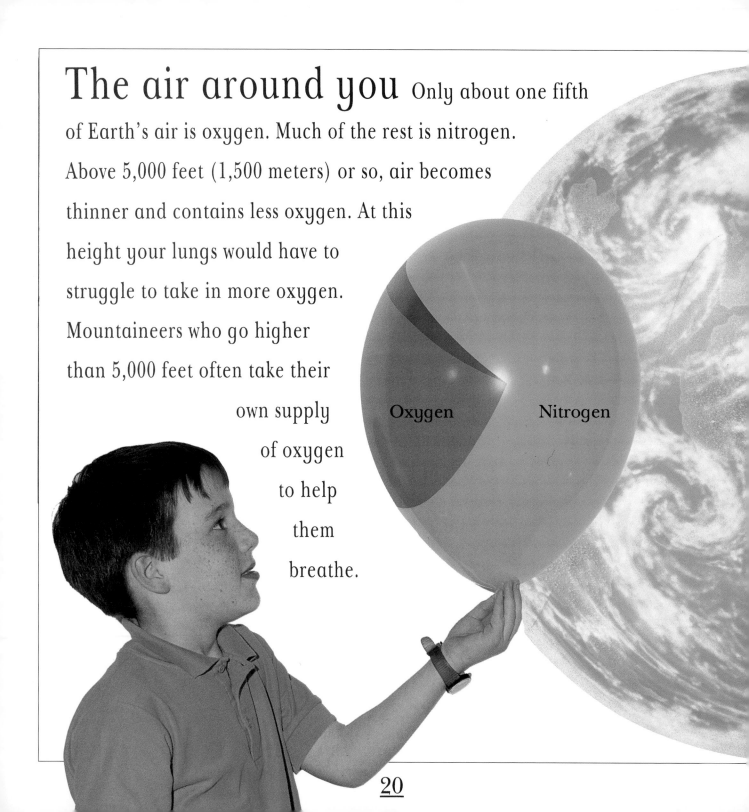

Oxygen

Nitrogen

Mountain dwellers' bodies are used to thinner air. This Nepalese farmer in the Himalayas does not need extra oxygen.

The higher you go, the thinner the air becomes. Out in space there is no air at all.

Just as too little oxygen can be harmful, so can too much. Breathing in pure oxygen for more than a few minutes would make you feel dizzy and faint.

Talking

Breathing is also used for talking. As you breathe out, air is pushed up your windpipe and into your voice box. Can you feel your adam's apple? Your voice box is just behind it.

Across the opening to your voice box are two pearly-pink ridges. These are your vocal cords. When air flows between the cords, they vibrate and make sounds.

You can stretch or loosen the cords to make higher or lower sounds.

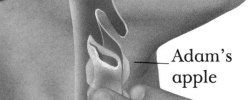

Adam's apple

The different positions of your tongue, teeth, cheeks and lips form the sounds into words.

The harder you breathe out, the louder the sounds. Take a deep breath. See how long you can whisper without taking another breath. Now try again – this time shouting. Because you use more breath to shout, you cannot keep going so long.

More sounds

You can make other sounds while breathing. You laugh by taking a deep breath in, then letting it out in a rat-tat-tat of short breaths. You cry in the same way. A yawn is an extra-deep breath in, a sigh is a long breath out.

Sneezes and coughs are noisy blasts of air that help get rid of dirt or mucus in your nose or air tubes. A sneeze can explode at a speed of more than 100 miles (160 kilometers) an hour!

Mucus is a sticky liquid which traps specks of dust and dirt. Tiny hairs in your air tubes, called cilia, gently sweep the mucus away from the lungs up to your nose or mouth to be sneezed or coughed out. A cough can also blow out food which has gone down the wrong way.

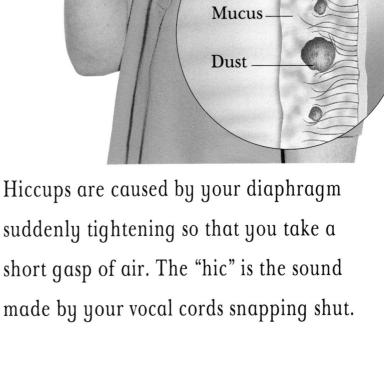

Cilia

Mucus

Dust

Hiccups are caused by your diaphragm suddenly tightening so that you take a short gasp of air. The "hic" is the sound made by your vocal cords snapping shut.

Breathing problems

There are many different reasons why people have breathing problems. People with asthma have very delicate bronchioles which sometimes close up and stop them from breathing out. Asthma sufferers use an inhaler to blow medicine into their bronchioles to keep them open.

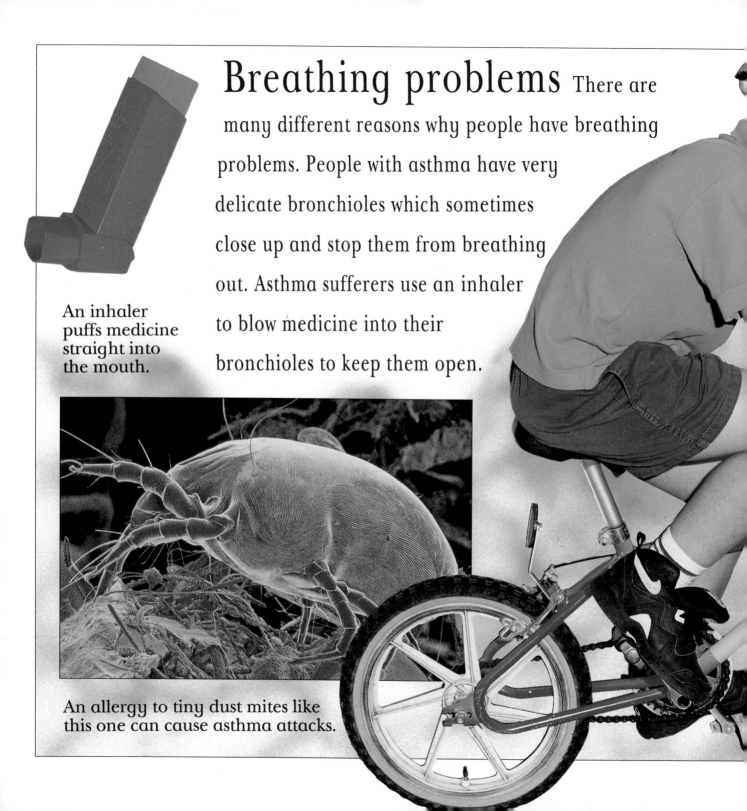

An inhaler puffs medicine straight into the mouth.

An allergy to tiny dust mites like this one can cause asthma attacks.

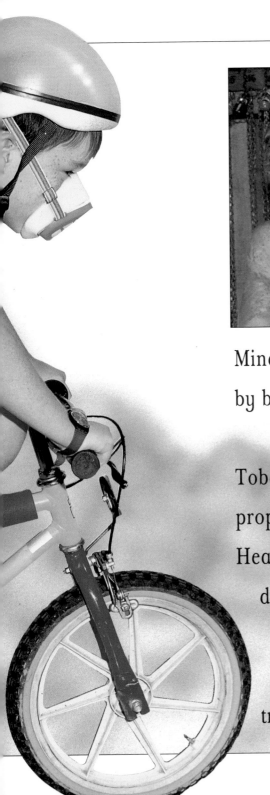

Miners sometimes suffer from chest complaints caused by breathing in dusty air every day.

Tobacco smoke stops a smoker's cilia from working properly so that mucus and dirt build up in the lungs. Heavy smokers often develop bad coughs and find it difficult to breathe easily.

Many cyclists now wear masks to help prevent traffic exhaust from damaging their lungs.

Did you know?

... that a pair of adult lungs weighs about 2.2 pounds (1 kilogram)?

... that an adult's lungs hold nearly 6 quarts (5 $\frac{1}{2}$ liters) of air? It would take you about three days to drink this amount of liquid.

... that the longest known attack of hiccuping, suffered by Iowan Charles Osborne, lasted continuously for 69 years, 5 months?

... that pearl divers in the Pacific Ocean can hold their breath for between two and three minutes at a time? DO NOT TRY THIS YOURSELF!

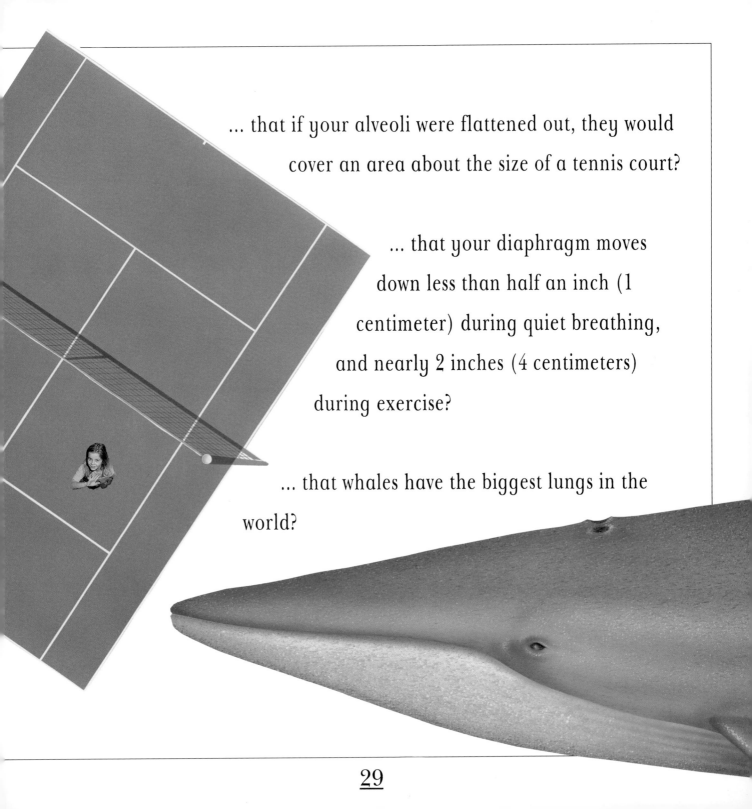

... that if your alveoli were flattened out, they would cover an area about the size of a tennis court?

... that your diaphragm moves down less than half an inch (1 centimeter) during quiet breathing, and nearly 2 inches (4 centimeters) during exercise?

... that whales have the biggest lungs in the world?

Index

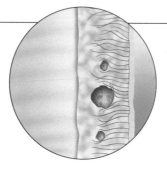